THE HUMOR AND WARMTH OF POPE JOHN XXIII

The Humor and Warmth of POPE JOHN XXIII

Originally "The Stories of Pope John XXIII"

HIS ANECDOTES AND LEGENDS

by Louis Michaels

A POCKET BOOKS SPECIAL
PUBLISHED BY POCKET BOOKS, INC.
New York 1965

The Humor and Warmth of Pope John XXIII
 This Pocket Book Special
is published by arrangement with Templegate
Publishers. Printed in the U.S.A.

THE HUMOR AND WARMTH OF POPE JOHN XXIII

One of the most frequently told stories about Pope John that circulated among members of the diplomatic corps was of his reminiscing about his peasant origin. "In Italy," he was fond of saying, "there are three ways of losing one's money—women, gambling, and farming. My father chose the most boring of the three."

✠

In World War I, Father Roncalli was drafted into the Medical Corps of the Italian Army and in what he later described as "a moment of weakness" grew a handsome black moustache. Six months later, clean shaven, he became a military chaplain. Years later, as Pope John XXIII, he received in audience a group of Italian bishops among whom was Bishop Arrigo Pintonello, the Chief Chaplain of the Italian Army.

The Pope strolled among the crimson throng and suddenly looked up at the beribboned chest of the Chief Chaplain. The Pope came swiftly to attention and gravely saluted. "Sergeant Roncalli reporting, Sir," he said.

All public figures have occasionally a need for privacy and protection from the simply curious. Pope Pius XI delighted in taking walks in the Vatican gardens from which on these occasions all workmen and visitors were barred. Pope Pius XII followed this practice of his predecessor. Even the tourists who might have witnessed from the heights of the dome of St. Peter's these lonely walks were told by Vatican guards that admittance to the dome was forbidden. Pope John often walked in the Vatican gardens but he cancelled the orders of Pius XII. "I don't want to be the ruler of a prison or a cemetery. Why shouldn't they look?" he asked the guards who were surprised at this breach of a twenty-year-old procedure, "I'm not doing anything scandalous." On another occasion he met a group of laborers in the gardens who had dropped their tools and prepared to withdraw when he approached. "Why are you doing this?" he asked. His assistant explained that it was for reasons of security. "But why?" the Pope asked, "I would not have hurt them."

✠

As Patriarch of Venice, Cardinal Roncalli dispensed with the ceremonial gondola and private launch and made use of the public transit system. Whenever possible he took the 'vaporetto' or public launch-bus. When this was not convenient he hired a taxi gondola. One day, making his way across St. Mark's Square in flood time he took a short cut through a cafe—the Birreria Leoncini—and the bartender looked up in surprise to see the Patriarch. He blurted out, "Want to wet your throat, Eminenza?" "No, nor my feet either," Cardinal Roncalli laughed, and he continued on his way.

An amused Pope John told newsmen that his own brother had made the best commentary on his election when the old Bergamo countryman wryly remarked: "So many men in our village have taken Holy Orders that according to the law of averages one of them had to become Pope."

The news of the election was not received in the same spirit by his sister Assunta who clapped her hands to her head and exclaimed: "My God, they've chosen little Angelo."

The great peasant bulk of Archbishop Roncalli was the delight of his Parisian friends who knew his consummate shrewdness as apostolic delegate and the dean of the diplomatic corps in the French capital. His enormous ears and large nose, his thick, stubby fingers, his wide and generous smile—the whole genial appearance of the man—seemed the antithesis of the story-book diplomat. He set one of the finest tables in Paris and hired as chef Roger, later the proprietor of the famous restaurant, *La Grenouille*. His charm became legendary. "He is," said Robert Schuman, author of the famous Schuman Plan, "the only man in Paris in whose company one feels a physical sensation of peace."

✠

A somber group of Venetians came in 1958 to pay their condolences to Cardinal Roncalli upon the death of Pope Pius XII, little knowing that their patriarch would be his successor. "Here, here," the Cardinal said, anxious to put them all at ease. "The Pope is dead but you must remember the old saying: *Morto un Papa se ne fa un altro!* (When a Pope dies they make another)."

One Christmas the Pope drove over to the Gesu Bambino Hospital to visit the sick children. Scores of photographers jostled one another and flash bulbs popped. "There are fourteen works of mercy that we recognize," John told the photographers. "Maybe we should add a fifteenth to the list —that of enduring people who are annoying. I am quite fond of photographers but I would like to have a little peace. But I don't want to make you practice this fifteenth work of mercy by listening to a long speech so I'll be brief." After his talk the Pope walked into the wards of the hospital. He stopped at one bed and bent over a small boy. "What's your name?" the Pope asked. The child explained that his name was a very long one with many saints in it but that now everybody called him Giuseppe. "And what is your name?" the child asked his visitor innocently. "Oh, my name is Giuseppe too," the Pope told him, "but now everybody calls me John."

L'Osservatore Romano is the most conservative of newspapers. It is given to the baroque rhetoric of the nineteenth century and has traditionally referred to the Pope in the exalted and flattering language of courtly grandeur. Quotations from the Pope are usually introduced by such phrases as: "We gather from the Holy Father's august lips," or "the illustrious and supreme Pontiff has said . . ." The morning after his election John telephoned the editor, Count Della Torre, waking him at 6:30, and asked that he come to see him. When Della Torre arrived, Pope John said, "We are living in the twentieth century. Let us have a style that suits the times and if you write simply 'the Pope has done this—the Pontiff has said that,' I would certainly prefer it." Then perhaps to take some of the sting from the reprimand he smiled and corrected himself: "*We* would prefer it."

Pope John's example of charity and integrity stemmed from the deep conviction that, as he himself put it, "It really does not matter what people think of me or say about me. I must remain true to my own resolution at any cost. I mean to be good and kind always to everybody."

On one of his auto trips through a certain Roman tenement district, John waved to the crowds who had in typical Roman greeting hung blankets and bright fabrics from their balcony railings and even over many of the bill-boards on his route. When he discovered that some of the flapping blankets covered large portraits of a sinuous and shapely movie actress, John was pleased at the consideration the tenement dwellers had shown in covering the advertisements but he rebuked them gently by saying, "It is good that you do this but you should realize that I am an old man and if one of my age is thought to be scandalized by pictures like these, what of yourselves and your children?"

John XXIII endeared himself to the Roman poor in a most personal way by his visits to their neighborhoods and his habit of reminding them of his own poor beginnings. In one such visit as they crowded around his open car he told them, "You have not come to see the son of a king, of an emperor, or one of the greats of this earth, but only a priest—a son of poor people, who was called by the Lord and carries the burden of being the Supreme Pontiff."

✠

Having grown up as the child of devout parents, Giuseppe Roncalli developed a love of the Madonna that is typical of the Italian country people. The festivals he remembered from his childhood in all probability centered on a procession in honor of the Virgin Mary and he realized the importance of these local devotions to the pilgrims who came to see him as Holy Father. Once a group of motorcyclists from Sardinia were received in an audience and Pope John, brushing past the typically rough and austere exterior of these islanders whose tradition is also the hospitable and honorable tradition of shepherds, said to them: "When you get to Cagliari, tell the Madonna of Bonaria [a 13th century gilded wood carving venerated by Sardinians in the Cathedral of Cagliari] that the Pope sent you, and tell her he asks that she will bless Italy, you and your families."

In the interval between his election and his coronation Pope John took a tour of his tiny Vatican State. He poked his head into the carpentry shop and, seeing a number of men bent over their lathes and saws, said: "This looks like thirsty work." He ordered wine for everyone and joined them in a toast.

Throughout his life Pope John kept a diary confiding to its pages his most intimate estimations of his own character. The diary was made public some months after his death and it gives us some insight into the heart of a man whom novelist Morris West has called 'this builder of bridges for us poor devils' and whom Sander Vanocur, the NBC television reporter, has called 'this powerful and good man.' "I intend to use joviality, pleasantness and happiness with all persons," John wrote, "but to act in seriousness and modesty, especially with those who have mistreated me."

He was in his early twenties when he wrote that he would try to imitate St. Francis Xavier in his denials of self, "resisting my personal inclinations and enduring a bit of suffering."

✠

Pope John's actions from the first moment of his election seemed to be those of a man who as his career in the church evolved had said to himself, "If I were Pope I would do thus and so." When in his old age he was in fact Pope he did all the things that seemed prudent and good in the time that was given to him. All men in authority feel a certain loneliness in their decisions, but none perhaps so much as one who arrives at this position and so advanced in years. He said that his sleep was often broken in the early days of his reign and he would waken with the thought: "I must speak with the Pope about this . . . But I *am* the Pope!" Then he would add: "Very well then, I shall speak to the Lord about it."

Through the years—from Cimabue and Giotto through El Greco to today—artists have sought the commission to paint a portrait of the Pope. An American artist, Bernard Godwin, obtained just such a commission in December, 1959, and Pope John at the end of his first sitting laughingly remarked, "Now I understand how the Saints felt when they were burned at the stake." After the portrait was completed Mr. Godwin recalled with enormous pleasure that from time to time he would find himself respectfully re-seating the subject or re-adjusting the folds of the Pope's garments, forgetting the tradition that no one touches the person of the Pope. "Every time I did so I heard muffled gasps from his secretary and valet but the Holy Father, hearing these reactions, smiled broadly and his eyes twinkled."

The former president of Ecuador was one of Pope John's early visitors and at the end of the audience the Pope told him that he would like to give him some souvenirs for his family. "I haven't been here long," John said, "and I don't have many personal things in the library here. You look in that drawer and I'll look in this one and we'll see what we can find. Ah! Here's something." He held up three medals struck in the reign of Pope Pius XII. "How many children have you?" he asked. "Five, your Holiness," the Ecuadorian replied. "Oh my!" Pope John said, "in that case I don't believe that we can help you. I can't find any more medals here. I tell you what—you must organize a raffle and the three children who win will get the medals."

The affection the French felt for the papal nuncio was a reciprocal one so far as Archbishop Roncalli was concerned. He loved the French and made their culture his own. From the first, according to many sources, he would quote their literature from the medieval troubadors to contemporary poets. The "Fables" of La Fontaine especially amused and inspired him. "In the tales of La Fontaine," he said, "we find ourselves in the intimate heart of everyone—from the men who govern to the diplomats, from great industrialists to the most lowly laborers, from artists of the greatest or of no fame, to the poorest of *clochards*. Everybody there discovers himself. And it is good for us to rest there awhile." Ending one of his popular New Year addresses to the President of the Republic, Vincent Auriol, he quoted a few lines from La Fontaine, and M. Auriol said, "I recognized La Fontaine in spite of the accent." "Thank you, Monsieur," replied Roncalli, "it took me a long time to get used to yours too."

Much of the ages-old papal protocol was a nuisance to John but he recognized the valid historical reasons behind it and he was not one who believed in change for the sake of change. "One of the humiliations we have had to endure as the successor of St. Peter," he said, "is to see men kneel to us. Our attendants used to kneel three times on arriving and departing. We have now agreed that they will genuflect only once in the morning and once at night." One American bishop kneeling to kiss the papal ring was drawn to his feet by the Holy Father and guided graciously to a comfortable chair. In the course of a lengthy conversation Pope John apologetically asked his visitor, "Would you mind if I had a cup of soup? I find that at my age I need some nourishment during the day."

If the Christian world heard with surprise in January, 1959, that Pope John wished to call together the bishops of the world in an Ecumenical Council, some of the Curia cardinals received the news with dismay. "We can't possibly hold a Council by 1963," said one member of the Curia. "All right," said John, "we'll have it in 1962 then."

"When the body gets worn out," Pope John once said, "the soul gets in shape."

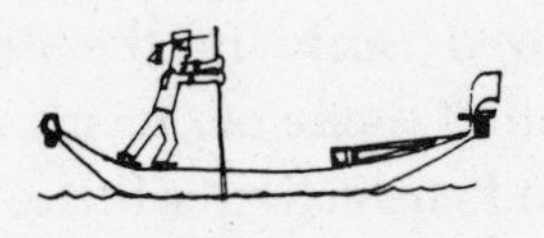

"They say I am a diplomat," he once told his Vicar General in Venice, "but the Church has only one diplomacy, the priesthood. This is the diplomacy I have always tried to practice." But he moved easily in the diplomatic world and summed up his policy as one of "seeing everything, overlooking a great deal and correcting a little."

✠

In the autumn of 1962, as Vatican Council II got under way, Pope John explained some of the delays to a group of bishops. "Nobody here knows how to run an ecumenical council. After all, none of us has ever been to one. It seems to me a council is like a new car. The first few miles you are breaking it in and have to go slowly or you will ruin the motor." But as the discussions and arguments went on, some correspondents reported Pope John's good humor was giving way to mild impatience, and that if the Council fathers did not make more rapid progress they would not be returning to their various sees for the Christmas season. Looking out over a chill and dismal St. Peter's Square one day in late November, the Pope turned to one of his attendants and with an enigmatic smile remarked, "What fun Christmas would be with all these Bishops here."

From the first days of his papacy, John XXIII was a man who liked change, not just for the sake of novelty (although one attendant is reported to have said, "if he were told the Pope could only walk on a carpet he would have all the carpets removed"), but change based on very practical considerations and motivated by a delightful imagination. In the drafty corridors of the Vatican palace and the high-ceilinged rooms where he lived it occured to John that not for centuries had Popes worn the *camauro,* the red velvet head covering we sometimes see in Renaissance portraits. Pope

John ordered one made for himself and wore it with great aplomb. He also asked that a white felt hat be made, since white was a cooler head covering in Italy's hot, mid-summer months. The red velvet shoes the popes traditionally wear he replaced with a pair of peasant's stout walking shoes, and he had these dyed red. He also saw no practical reason to reserve the elaborately embroidered ceremonial stole for solemn occasions and wore it for the most ordinary events, although its magnificence had not been designed to flatter his short two-hundred-pound frame.

It is easy to imagine the joy Pope John gave to the children of Bambino Gesu Hospital when after his illness in 1962 his first visit outside the Vatican was to them on Christmas day. They had prayed with the Sisters for his recovery and when he came to see them he spent close to an hour visiting with almost every child. As is so often the case with old men, Pope John could talk easily with the very young and to these little invalids he said encouragingly, "You see I'm in perfect condition. Oh, I'm not quite able to run any races but I am well again. At any rate I'm feeling well."

"In every case," he said, "I aim for that which unites rather than that which separates. We are all in accord. Our natural principles can take us down the same street. For the best thing is mutual confidence."

At the conclusion of one of his audiences during which much laughter had filled the hall the Holy Father said: "Now let us pray for you, for your families and also for the Pope—because to tell the truth, I want to live a long time—yes, I like to live."

A priest owns no more personal possession than his breviary, the compilation of obligatory daily prayers and psalms. When Pope John received in audience an Anglican priest, Canon Donald Rea, the Vicar of the Church of Sts. Peter and Paul in Eye, Suffolk, and the chairman of the Anglican Confraternity of Unity, he noticed that Canon Rea was carrying a worn and well-thumbed breviary. John said to the interpreter: "That breviary he is carrying looks a bit old. Mine is not new but it is newer than his. I will give him mine." The next day the Pope's breviary was delivered to Canon Rea, the silk bookmarks showing where John had completed his office on the previous day, the Feast of the Sacred Heart. The leather volumes bore the insignia of the Cardinal

Patriarch of Venice and scattered throughout the pages Canon Rea discovered many memorial cards asking for prayers for members of the Roncalli family.

"Treat temptation like flies," John said. "Brush it away . . . If the priest burns as if with fire and therefore gives off a splendid light, pure and ardent, he is beyond price. If not, he counts for little."

Pope John's love for all mankind was apparent in every phase of his public life, and his fatherly concern for the people he received in audience was reported over and over again by the great and ordinary who visited him. On the closing day of the first session of the Vatican Council as the great bells of St. Peter's rang out the noon Angelus John appeared at the open window of his study to bless the thousands in the square below. Nuns and taxi-drivers, tourists and shop-keepers as well as several hundred purple-robed prelates mingled happily within the arms of Bernini's colonade. As an attendant placed a red velvet cape around the Pontiff's shoulders for protection against the bracing air, Pope John said with spontaneous and obvious delight: "Look at them—the whole family is here!"

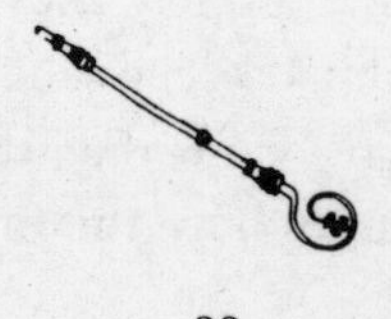

For more than a century it had been traditional for the Pope to eat alone. But Pope John was a gregarious man and liked to share his pleasures. For a week or more he tried to observe the tradition but finally he gave up and invited Monsignor Capovilla to eat with him. "To have to eat alone makes me feel like a seminarian being punished," the Pope said. He later included some of his old friends as his dinner companions and told them, "I get no pleasure out of eating alone with Capovilla. He eats like a canary." Sometime after this Pope John told one of his old friends, "I am all for tradition, but my resolution to eat alone didn't last over eight days. After all, nothing in scripture says that I must eat alone. Besides it's much better this way."

Archbishop Roncalli when he was papal nuncio in Paris seldom let his fellow members of the diplomatic corps forget that his first calling was to the service of God. "My position in France is comparable to St. Joseph's place in Our Lord's life. I am to be the guardian of Our Saviour and his prudent protector."

✠

At the outbreak of the second World War, Archbishop Roncalli was the Vatican envoy to neutral Turkey. A special service for peace was held in the Cathedral of Istanbul and the Archbishop concluded his prayer with these words, so typical of the attitude for which he later became so famous: "We ask peace of Thee in behalf of all those who live under this same sky whatever their race may be, for we are all brothers no matter what our religion, our ethical customs, our traditions or social position."

"I am Pope John," he once said, "not because of any personal merit but because of an act of God, and God is in everyone of us. I am Pope John and Nikita Khrushchev is Nikita Khrushchev. I don't see why I should think that God shows the truth only through me."

Pope John had his own favorite stories of the Council and several times told visitors what one of his predecessors, Pius XI, had said about ecumenical councils. "In a council there are three periods: that of the devil, who tries to mix up the papers; that of man, who helps with the confusion; and finally, that of the Holy Spirit, who clears up everything."

✠

Gentle manners came naturally to John and he found the use of the imperial 'We' rather alien to his open and warm-hearted personal approach to people. He could not refrain from taking his visitors by the arm and escorting them to the door when they were to leave. His chief of protocol, the Master of the Chamber, told him that because of his position he should not himself open doors and stand aside while others preceded him. "Why not?" Pope John said, "it is a courteous gesture and I've always done it." "But you are now Pope," the Master of the Chamber objected, "and protocol forbids it." "Very well," the Pope replied, "I still think it's absurd but you undoubtedly know best about these things." For weeks thereafter John referred to the Master of the Chamber as "our charming jailer."

"When you are charitable you are sure of never being mistaken. Learn how to understand, to forgive, to be gracious. That's Christianity. By contrast, it is the way of the world to push, to parade, to use violence. That's all wrong. The force we possess is the truth and the charity of Jesus Christ."

The Pope often left his desk to take unannounced walks to the most unlikely spots in Vatican City. He once dropped in to see the Vatican radio station at an hour when only one operator was on duty. The flustered man jumped to his feet when he saw the stout man in white wandering through the corridors. He nervously explained that he was alone and that the rest of the staff would be back shortly. "That's all right," said Pope John, "I'll come back some other time." He went on some time later to look in on the carpenter shop. To one of the workers there, a generously padded man, John said: "I see that you belong to the same party that I do." "But, Holy Father, I don't belong to any party," the man replied. "Yes, you do," said Pope John, "you become a member automatically—it's the Fat Man's Party."

When someone told Pope John that he seemed to be losing weight, John said: "No, I'm really not, but do you know what I do when I begin to feel that I'm getting too fat? I go over and stand next to Cicognani [the stoutest cardinal] and I feel then that I am as thin as a rail."

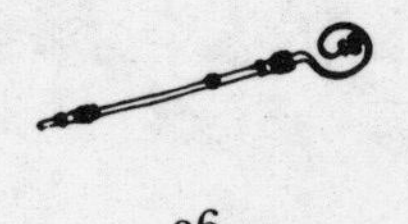

"He was truly a father to all men," one of the Protestant observers at the Vatican Council said. This observer had been particularly impressed by his statement that, "we do not intend to conduct a trial of the past. We do not want to prove who was right and who was wrong. All we want to say is, Let us come together. Let us make an end to our divisions."

He once told a Jewish boy who had been baptized a Catholic to continue to support his Jewish community and added, "By becoming a Catholic you do not become less a Jew."

After reciting the Angelus prayer at the papal summer residence at Castel Gandolfo Pope John was told of the Russian astronaut then circling the earth. "Let us pray for this man," the Pope said, "that he may be successful and that he may return to earth safely."

The protocol surrounding audiences with the Pope is unnerving to many of his visitors and John XXIII did all that he could to relieve the stiffness of these occasions. Even with those who were quite equal to the formality of the ceremony of being received in his red-carpeted library the Pope would have a gracious but informal manner. He interrupted one ambassador at a pause in his eloquent presentation of credentials to say: "Your Excellency, let us hand over these formal speeches to our secretaries and you and I will go to my office and have a quiet talk." It was this same desire to put others at their ease that prompted him to ask his secretary's advice on how to address Mrs. John F. Kennedy, when the American First Lady paid him a visit. Monsignor Capovilla suggested the Holy Father could address her as Mrs. Kennedy, according to American custom, or as Madame because her ancestry was French. While waiting, Pope John tried both forms several times quietly to himself and when the President's wife was shown into his library he stood up and holding out his hands in welcome he cried: "Jacqueline."

✠

En route to Rome from Poland after his release from a Communist jail, Cardinal Wyszynski stopped off at Venice to see his old friend Cardinal Roncalli who met him at the Mestre railroad station during the train's forty-five minute stopover. "I will show you our beautiful city," the Patriarch said. He took the Polish Cardinal to a motor launch and the two priests went for a tour through the city. Wyszynski, delighted by the lacy Venetian architecture and the fluid beauty of the canals, was not attentive to the time. In the great square of St. Mark he saw the clock tower where the Moorish figures have been striking the time for more than five hundred years. He abruptly reminded Roncalli that his train was about to leave and that he would have to go immediately. "You must not worry," the Cardinal of Venice said. "Notice that man sitting at the rear of the launch. He is the station master at Mestre. So long as he is with us the train can not leave. I prevailed upon him to join us and nothing leaves here without his permission."

"My dear man," Pope John once said to an American bishop, "when you face Jesus Christ in eternity he is not going to ask you how you got along with the Roman Curia but how many souls you saved."

To the dismay of many of the personnel at the Vatican in the early days of his pontificate John XXIII displayed a most carefree sense of his own dignity. Once seeing himself in a full length mirror, he chuckled happily and said: "O Lord, this man is going to be a disaster on television."

✠

Archbishop Roncalli tried to master the language of each country to which he was assigned. Shortly after he was sent as Apostolic Delegate to Turkey he said: "If in Rome Christ is a Roman, in Turkey he must become a Turk," and proceeded to gain a speaking knowledge of the Turkish language.

The traditionally conservative cardinals in the Roman Curia were less than pleased to hear of John's intention to call an ecumenical council of the world's bishops. They received the news with the same enthusiasm with which a bank looks forward to the arrival of the examiners and did everything within their power to see that the preparatory commissions were well supplied with Curia representatives. John, biding his time, did not interfere. He did, however, defeat much of the maneuvering by having his trusted private secretary, Monsignor Capovilla, quietly move behind the scenes to let any cardinals, doubtful of John's position, know his mind in the affair. "*Sono nel sacco qui* (I'm in a bag here)," he said to Cardinal Cushing.

The Council convened on schedule and the Pope watched its proceedings on a closed circuit television system set up in his private apartment. He followed every argument and defended the Council against those curial critics who felt that such public disagreements were an embarrassment to the Church. "Let them continue," John said, "after all, we're not friars singing in a choir."

Pope John's wit was more apparent to the Italians than to those in the audiences who relied on the translated interpretations following his addresses. This was particularly true of his puns which were subtle and peppered many of his talks.

Several members of his staff were old friends from a time before his Venetian days. Among them were Monsignor Dell' Acqua who had been with him in Turkey, and Cardinal Canali who had been a friend of former years and had the distinction of having crowned him with the triple tiara.

Shortly after his coronation a visitor asked him if he was enjoying Rome as much as he had liked Venice. John lightly replied, "It's not so different. I'm still surrounded by Acqua and Canali."

✠

Pope John, with the Italian's love of music and proverb, summarized the achievement of the opening session of his Vatican Council with these words, "The first session was like the slow and majestic prelude to a great masterpiece. *Chi va piano, va sano.* (He who goes slowly, goes safely.)"

The French minister of foreign affairs, Robert Schuman, once took the floor of the National Assembly to rebuke a deputy who had, to the amazement of his colleagues, harsh words for the popular papal nuncio. Drawing Schuman aside after his speech, Archbishop Roncalli thanked him for his defense and added, "I am even more grateful that you said nothing which would hurt Monsieur—————," the deputy who had attacked him.

The Pope is customarily carried into St. Peter's Basilica on the *sedia gestatoria,* the portable throne borne on the shoulders of twelve footmen. Shortly after his election one of his old friends told John of his great pride at seeing a man from Bergamo raised high above the crowds in such solemn procession. How did Pope John feel about all this? "Well, it's pretty windy up there," the new Pope said. Moreover it reminded him of his boyhood days when his father swung him up on his shoulders during a parade. It was from just such a height and on that very occasion that he decided to become a priest.

A priest once rushed up to Pope John as the Pope was getting out of his car to take a walk near Vatican City. He begged the Pope to pray for the paralyzed wife of a friend. "We can do more than that," the Pope said and re-entering his car had his driver take him directly to the house of the paralyzed woman where he chatted for some time, to the great delight of the invalid and her family.

The presence of a clergyman at the international dinners for the envoys of foreign governments in the French capital often created a certain uneasiness among those who wished to protect their good friend from embarrassment when certain feminine guests arrived in gowns more fashionable than modest in design. It was suggested that word be quietly passed to some of the offending ladies but Archbishop Roncalli, hearing of the plan, said that it would perhaps be better in this instance to ignore it. "I have found," he added, "that on such occasions it is not so much the woman at whom the crowd is looking, but at me to see my reaction."

The Sistine Chapel is ordinarily reserved for the most solemn religious ceremonies. It is there that popes are elected and John, with his unerring sense of the dramatic, thought that it should be used for other purposes as well. The representatives of seventy-five governments and more than a dozen international organizations were summoned to a special audience with the new Pope the day after the opening of the first session of the Vatican Council. He received them seated on a throne in the Sistine Chapel in front of Michelangelo's fresco of *The Last Judgement*. At one point in his address he pointed to the great work behind him: "Look there at this vast masterpiece of Michelangelo, the seriousness of which gives cause for thought and reflection. We must indeed render an account to God—we and all the heads of state who bear responsibility for the fate of nations . . . In all conscience let them give ear to the anguished cry of 'Peace, Peace,' which rises up to Heaven from every part of the world, from innocent children and from those grown old . . . May this thought of the reckoning that they are to face spur them to make every effort toward achieving this blessing which for the human family is a greater blessing than any other."

✠

His great love for his family and his affectionate memories of Bergamo colored many of John's conversations and at the most unlikely times. As the first session of the Vatican Council drew to a close some Bishops, tired from work and looking forward to returning to their homes, asked the Holy Father what he would like to do after the Council. He answered, "Spend a day tilling the fields with my brothers."

Even as nuncio the future Pope possessed a wit more soothing than scathing. One day a carpenter was called to put up a new bookcase in the Paris nunciature. When he accidentally hammered his thumb instead of a nail his awareness of the fact was broadcast in blasphemous terms. He invoked the witness of God and a procession of saints. Roncalli rose from his desk, walked into the next room where the carpenter was still licking his bruised thumb. "*Alors, qu'est-ce que c'est que ça? Vous ne pouvez pas dire 'merde' comme tout le monde?*" the nuncio asked.

Pope John ardently wished to learn English. He talked familiarly with his world-wide family in Italian, French and several middle Eastern languages but it was his great regret that he knew so little of the tongue used by millions of Christians. He set about the task of teaching himself by taking a book for which Cardinal Amleto Cicognani, the former apostolic delegate to Washington, had written an introduction and the Pope translated the introduction into Italian.

Some time after this he tried a five hundred word speech in English to the American students at the North American College: "So I am old," he said, "but in the English language I am still a baby—I am a child taking the first steps and please help me along."

Later he told a group of Americans that he hoped to talk to them "in the American language on our next visit—or anyway in Paradise where we will all speak the same language."

✠

Guido Gusso, Pope John's Venetian chauffeur, was as devoted to the new Pontiff as any of his aides. He drove the black Mercedes-Benz through the narrow Roman streets as the police escorts tried to form an orderly way for the car's progress and excited Romans pushed into the road to greet their bishop. He was particularly proud that his beloved passenger would talk to the crowds not in the exalted and formal language of ecclesiastical discourse but in their own familiar idiom. He told of driving Pope John into a predominantly Communist area of the city when the Pope, besieged by applauding crowds, clapped his hands to his head and, lapsing into idiomatic Italian, laughed, "I've really had to go some to get down here and this is a triumph."

It was not long after his election that members of the Vatican staff attending Pope John became aware that the new Pope rarely said: "I want." He used instead the gentler: "The way it looks to me."

More than thirty years before he became Pope he wrote to a friend that whereas there was something to be said for the motto of the ancients—"*Frangar non flectar* (I will break but not bend)"—he preferred to take as his own motto the reverse of the old one—"*Flectar non frangar* (I will bend but not break)"—"especially," he added, "when it comes to matters of a practical nature and I think that I am in line with the great tradition of the Church here."

✠

While he was Patriarch of Venice, Cardinal Roncalli suggested that several marble panels in the basilica of St. Mark be removed to give a better view of the altar to the faithful. He was opposed by the government commission on fine arts and, rather than allow the issue to become a bitter wrangle, the Patriarch quietly dropped the matter. "I do not want to force solutions," he said. "I only want anyone who thinks differently to be convinced of the good intention behind my proposal."

"I have had a hard time getting to sleep," Pope John told newsmen a week or so after his election, "so I've been reading the newspapers, not because I'm vain but just because I'm curious. I've been reading about the Council and have found hardly two stories that were correct in their reporting. I've read of holy Popes, diplomatic Popes, of political Popes, but really the Pope is only the Pope, a good shepherd who tries to defend truth and goodness."

In the rugged countryside east of Rome, St. Benedict and his sister St. Scholastica founded twelve little monasteries where more than one thousand years ago Benedict wrote his great monastic rule. The austerity of the surroundings and the strictness of St. Benedict's rule were no deterrent to the enthusiasm of the monks and the faithful who greeted the Holy Father when he made a visit to the monastery. "It is easy to see," John said, "that it has been some time since a Pope came here. I beg you to be good and orderly. Otherwise, they will never let me back into the Vatican."

When designs were submitted to Pope John for his coat of arms he chose the same figures he had used when he was Patriarch of Venice—the Roncalli tower and the Lion of St. Mark. Now the artist added the triple tiara and the Keys of St. Peter. Pope John approved the basic design but, pointing a stubby finger at the lion, he said: "Let's change his expression. Please don't make my lion look so cross."

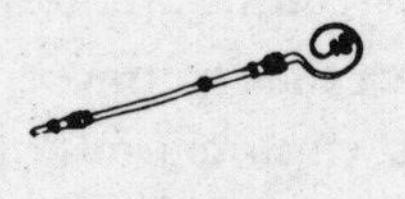

The people of Venice were delighted at the election of their Patriarch to the papacy but they must have felt a twinge of sadness at the separation this necessarily involved. Many thousands of them journeyed to Rome to be present at his coronation. While addressing their delegation, John changed in mid-speech from his pure Italian to their Venetian dialect and they roared their approval and interrupted his words with their lengthy applause. "If you start that kind of thing," he said, "this audience will never end. So please, don't interrupt me—" and then with a laugh he remembered the papal plural and added—"I mean *us!*"

Nikita Khrushchev's son-in-law, Alexei Adzhubei, came to Rome in the course of an official tour and Pope John astonished his Vatican staff by receiving the Russian and his wife in private audience. They were quite unprepared for such a warm reception and Rada Adzhubei murmured to her husband that he should look closely at the Pope's hands—"the beautiful hands of a Russian peasant." She was not aware of John's familiarity with Slavic languages and some time after the visit John told a friend, "How very nice of her to say this—my hands really are those of a peasant." The Pope suggested a tour of the Vatican apartments and he pointed out some of the more unusual decorations for his visitors. He asked Rada to say the names of her children—"It is good to hear their names from you for the names of children have a special sound from the lips of their own mothers." He then gave her a rosary, telling her that this age-old devotion reminded him of the prayer his mother used to recite with the family around the fire when he was a boy.

In the library Alexei got down to the political realities, bringing up the matter of inaugurating diplomatic relations between the Vatican and the Kremlin. John was appreciative of the delicacy of the problem but had a word of caution for the young Russian envoy. "You are a journalist, so you know the Bible and the progression of the work of Creation. You know that the Lord took six days for the work of Creation before coming to man. But as you also know, the days of the Bible are long and are really not days but epochs. Now we are at the first day. We meet one another, we look into one another's eyes and we see light there. Today is the first day—*Fiat lux*. The light is in your eyes and in mine. The Lord, if he wishes, will let us know the road to follow, but this will take some time. Right now we can only hope and pray."

As Adzhubei and his wife were preparing to leave, Pope John bade them farewell, saying, "I know that you call yourselves atheists but I hope that you will accept the blessing of an old man for your children at home."

Later that day, according to Monsignor Capovilla, John made this entry in his diary: "It may be a delusion, or it may be a mysterious thread of providence that I, as Pope, do not have the right to break."

✠

A Life Magazine reporter has told of John's great effectiveness in extemporaneous talks with the pilgrims who flocked to see him from all parts of the world. At one of his audiences at the papal summer residence—Castel Gandolfo, in the Alban Hills near Rome—he was talking to a large throng when a baby began to cry. The Pope interrupted his discourse to say, "Now don't you fret, bambino, I'll have a word for you too by and by." He finished reciting the Angelus with the crowd and then remembered the baby. "Here now," the Pope said, "is my word for you, bambino. Every night I say the third decade of the rosary for all the babies born in the last 24 hours because you are the treasure of the future."

John's direct answers were never given impulsively—a result perhaps of his long years in diplomatic society—but he was never evasive. A short time after his coronation he was asked a question of such a nature as to require a certain delicacy of framing in its answer. "Ask me that some other time," he said. "I'm not broken in yet."

Cardinal Roncalli spent part of his summers in Sotto il Monte when he was Patriarch of Venice. On one occasion, having blessed the grape harvest of his former neighbors, he added with his characteristic humor: "I hope that you will send me some of this wine when I go back to my lagoon. With all that water I'll be needing it."

✠

One of the American delegates to UNESCO (United Nations Educational, Scientific and Cultural Organization) often met Archbishop Roncalli when the papal nuncio was the Vatican's first permanent observer at the Organization. "In private talks," the American reported, "at the dinner table or at small receptions people seemed to remember what the nuncio said. Even the Russians had praise for him because he did not give them pious lectures. They made no great rush to the nearest Church to be baptized but I am sure that the seeds which Archbishop Roncalli planted will bear fruit."

Archbishop Roncalli, having caught a bad cold during the Christmas season of 1946, found himself voiceless on New Year's Eve. As papal nuncio it was his place to bring greetings to the government on behalf of the diplomatic corps. He chose one of his colleagues to read his address but his good nature and holiday mood bubbled over and he stood nearby and with appropriate gestures "gave" his speech in pantomime.

On Christmas Day, 1934, in a farewell broadcast to the Bulgarian people whom he was leaving after ten years of service as the Vatican's representative, he said: ". . . my beloved brothers, do not forget me, who will always remain beyond wind and sea the fervent friend of Bulgaria . . . my Bulgarian brothers, you have only to enter to find in my house the warmest and most affectionate hospitality."

✠

When the sixty-three year old Archbishop Roncalli began his brilliant term in Paris, few Parisians realized what a master of diplomacy had been sent to them. With his natural talent for hospitality and with the aid of his famous French chef, he became one of the most popular men in the city. Invitations to his lunches and dinners were eagerly sought after, not only for the fine food and wine and good cigars but for the brilliant conversation he seemed always to inspire. One member of the diplomatic corps said: "Roncalli was a master of diplomacy who never said anything he had not planned to say." And a Venetian who knew him later recalled that his "graceful conversation was like lace work or subtle embroidery." The Noble prize-winning novelist, François Mauriac, remarked on his "exquisite finesse." But the papal nuncio to Paris was unaffected by such praise. "I want to be remembered," he said, "only as a loyal and peaceful priest."

Pope John's witty way of identifying himself with those he received in audiences was not always an easy accomplishment. At one audience he welcomed a group of refrigerator salesmen by saying, "You are welcome though our jobs are distinct and far apart. Ours is to warm hearts." And when a United States Congressman, Brooks Hays, was presented to Pope John, Mr. Hays said quite unexpectedly, "I'm a Baptist." "Well, I'm John," said the Holy Father.

On November 4, 1958, at the Solemn Pontifical Mass which preceded his coronation as Sovereign Pontiff, John XXIII gave an unexpected sermon in which he asked for prayers and outlined briefly his ideas of the kind of Pope he wanted to be. "Some hope to find a skilled diplomat or a statesman, others a scholar or an organizer . . . or one whose mind is in touch with every form of modern knowledge . . . none of them is on the right track . . . the new Pope has before his mind the wonderful picture drawn by St. John, in the words of the Saviour himself, of the Good Shepherd."

✠

Pacem in Terris and *Mater et Magistra* are perhaps two of the most important church documents of modern times. Both of them were written by Pope John. They will not, however, be the most remembered things about this remarkable man. His cordiality and open-handed geniality were the virtues which drew all persons of whatever rank to him. He took no side in international affairs, conscious of his position, and he said in one of his audiences, "Since the Lord has placed me, poor man that I am, in His great service, I feel that I do not belong to anything particular in life—family, country, nation—even to projects that may be good—the world is my family." The seeds of ecumenism apparently began to bloom during his years in the Balkans when he met an old Armenian priest. "He left a deep impression on my soul," Pope John told friends later, "when he said to me, 'Excellency, one reads in the Gospels that our Lord pardons all sins save one that will be forgiven neither in Heaven nor here on earth. And what is that sin—is it not the division of the Church?' "

"Always respect everyone's dignity whatever his position," Pope John said. "Especially must we respect everyone's liberty, for God himself renders that."

The rules governing the conclave gathered for the election of a Pope are strict and guided by an undeviating protocol. Until officially dismissed by the new Pope the cardinals are required to remain in confinement. When John was elected he asked the cardinals to remain in session for a short time after the announcement of their choice so that he might talk to them later at leisure. But many cardinals, anxious to see the new Pope's first blessing to the City of Rome and to the world beyond, rushed to the windows and looked out upon the hundreds of thousands thronging the great square of St. Peter's. When Pope John returned to the cardinals he confronted the assembly gravely and announced that they had all been guilty of violating the rules of the conclave and were consequently subject to excommunication. His expression changed and he smiled as he added, "but in our new position we believe we are able to help you."

✠

The delegates from EURATOM, a council of representatives from six European nations for the development of peaceful uses of atomic energy, came to Rome and were received in audience by Pope John. Monsignor Capovilla, before their coming, tried to instruct the Pope so that he could talk more or less knowingly with his visitors. In the course of the audience, one of the EURATOM men, explaining a technical detail, went far beyond the comprehension of his distinguished host. The Pope thanked the man for his explanation and with a smile added, "I have really understood very little of what you have just said." Pointing to Capovilla, he said, "Last night my friend here prepared a lesson for me. I didn't understand that either. It is enough for me to know that six men can sit around a table in a spirit of peace and on that table I place my benediction." Newsmen in the group reported that some members of the delegation were so deeply moved that they were close to tears.

When Archbishop Roncalli was made a cardinal, his close friend, Vincent Auriol, the President of France and a convinced agnostic, asked if he might invoke an ancient privilege and, as head of a nominally Christian nation, present the red hat to the Archbishop in a private ceremony. So many members of the diplomatic corps, so many other friends, asked to attend that the affair grew quite beyond the proportions originally set for it. Roncalli said that he would like to have his brothers come from their Italian farm to see the ceremony and the three countrymen arrived in Paris, obviously ill at ease in the fashionable French capital and the high-ceilinged embassies. The morning after their arrival the Archbishop's limousine drew up before the front entrance of the nunciature to take them on a sight-seeing tour of the city. But the brothers were not yet ready.

"Will you help us tie our neckties?" one of the brothers asked the Archbishop.

"But weren't you wearing them?" he asked, "when you arrived yesterday? Who tied them for you then?"

"Assunta tied them for us before we left," Zaverio said.

"Well, then," the new cardinal replied, "let's forget the ties. We peasants mustn't put on airs. I don't wear one either," and he pointed to his clerical collar. The four brothers went off on their tour without ties. But the next day, the day of the ceremony, a thoughtful brother provided the visitors with formal clothes and snap-on ties so that they would feel more comfortable among the properly dressed diplomats who gathered to see the French president place the crimson biretta on the head of Giuseppe Cardinal Roncalli.

Pope John enjoyed planning pleasant surprises for those around him. Within three weeks of his election he asked Cardinal Tardini, acting or pro-secretary of state, to call together all the members of the secretariat of state for a special audience. They were presented to him and he talked with them quite informally. When they had all relaxed he became serious and said, "We find ourselves delayed and hampered by prefixes and suffixes and we are going to abolish as many as possible. We will begin by omitting the 'pro' from Monsignor Tardini's title and simply refer to him as 'Secretary of State for the Holy See.'" Cardinal Tardini until that moment had been unaware that he was to be promoted to the full title and office which he had until then held on a temporary basis.

Part of Cardinal Roncalli's building program in Venice was a new minor seminary. The old seminary had been housed in a beautiful villa which previous patriarchs had used as a country retreat. In order to help finance the new seminary Cardinal Roncalli sold the villa. A friend reminded him that he would be foregoing many quiet days and peaceful nights if he gave up this lovely property. The Cardinal replied: "I realize how lovely it is but, as a matter of fact, I sleep perfectly well in Venice. The seminary and the needs of the diocese are much more important. What counts is the salvation of souls."

There is more than one legend surrounding Archbishop Roncalli's appointment as nuncio to Paris. One of the most typical is that he was unable to decode the telegram that called him to the position and he misplaced it among other papers. Receiving no reply, the Vatican sent him another message and he referred to this later as "how I became a nuncio quite by accident." In a letter to a friend after the announcement of his appointment he said, "Where there are no horses, donkeys will do."

An Irishman, Father Thomas Ryan, was sent by the Vatican to be Bishop Roncalli's secretary when he represented the Holy See in Turkey. Father Ryan was a tall, raw-boned Celt and he and the sturdy Italian bishop became close friends. Bishop Roncalli delighted in teasing the good-natured Irishman and, after he became Pope, appointed Father Ryan to his personal staff. They often joked that the little English which Pope John learned came out in an Irish brogue. But in Turkey, Bishop Roncalli noticed that Father Ryan was less than politic in his references to those the Irish traditionally refer to as "left-handers." Roncalli regarded his assistant with good humor. "You Irish are impossible," he said. "The moment you come into the world, even before you are baptized, you begin damning everybody who doesn't belong to the Church, especially Protestants."

"I'm not really a diplomat," Archbishop Roncalli once said, "or if I am one I am so only incidentally for I try to speak nothing but the truth. Perhaps it is this which leads people to credit me with diplomacy."

One of the first chiefs of state whom Pope John received after his coronation was Canadian Premier John Diefenbaker. The Pontiff shrugged, threw up his hands and exclaimed: "Well, here I am at the end of the road and the top of the heap."

As Patriarch of Venice, Cardinal Roncalli had a number of bishops under his jurisdiction. One of these, Bishop Augusto Gianfrancheschi, had the reputation of being a strict and most rigid disciplinarian. The diocese of Casena required a bishop and Gianfrancheschi was appointed to the see. Many of the clergy in that diocese were unhappy with the appointment and some of the disaffected distributed mourning cards with black edges announcing the choice. Cardinal Roncalli had no course except to reprimand those who had perpetrated the trick but he let his feelings be known privately. "If that fellow Gianfrancheschi had been present at the Creation he would have pitched in to help God make the world," the Cardinal said.

Referring to his days in the diplomatic corps, John XXIII once said: "A good table and a good cellar are great assets."

The Soviet representative in France when Archbishop Roncalli was in Paris was Ambassador Bogomolov—"a civilized, courteous and really fine person," according to the Archbishop. But Roncalli felt more closely drawn to Edouard Herriot, the former premier of France and a bristling anti-clerical. The two were often seen together and Herriot was fond of saying that if all priests were like his friend Roncalli there would be no anti-clericalism. In one gathering the subject of Masonry and its influence on French politics occupied their attention. "Here's a question for you, Excellency," Roncalli joked. "You're a good Mason." Herriot told a story about remaining for the full course of a cabinet meeting some years before even though many of the cabinet officers had left to attend a lodge meeting. "I may yet be around to serve your Mass," the Archbishop laughed. It was only a short time later that Herriot on his death-bed asked for the last sacraments of the church.

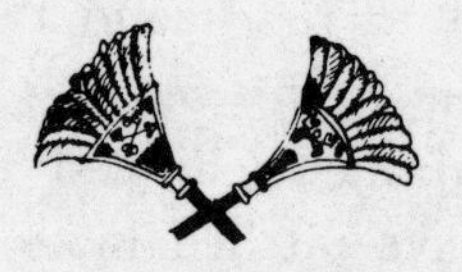

John's humility was rooted in his charity but he was never guilty of false humility. He knew that he was talked about throughout the world, that not only members of his own faith but countless millions of other denominations looked toward him with affection and reverence. "We need not boast before God," he said, "but if all these manifestations are not an illusion of self-esteem but rather something really corresponding to reality, then this is the right moment to enliven our courage and religious zeal and to do our best to apply God's precepts on earth."

✠

Just as he thought a good table and good manners were welcome parts of good living, John XXIII considered grooming an important part of the priestly image. When as Patriarch of Venice he noticed that a priest who often called on him was usually unshaved, rather than embarrass him by calling his attention to it directly he sent the man an electric razor.

Among his Jewish friends John felt both at home and at ease. "I am Joseph your brother," he told a group of Jews who had come to see him. At another meeting when he was praised for his many quotations from the Law and the Prophets he teased: "Of course I know the Old Testament, but we all know the law and when it comes to a matter of testaments it is the last one that really counts."

For centuries the liturgy of Holy Week had made reference to 'the perfidious Jews'. The phrase had been unhappily translated from the Latin which in its root sense means 'unbelieving'. It had, nevertheless, been a source of embarrassment and division and one of John's first liturgical amendments was his directive to remove the offending adjective.

When, as apostolic delegate to Turkey, Archbishop Roncalli was approached by Franz von Papen, the German ambassador, the normally cordial, diplomatic atmosphere was chilled by the icily formal attitude of the Vatican envoy. Von Papen wondered if perhaps Rome could be persuaded to issue a statement condemning the atheistic Communists whom the German armies were so valiantly fighting. Roncalli demurred. "What shall I tell them," he asked, "about the millions of Jews your countrymen are murdering in Germany and in Poland?"

Although the motorcycle police who were assigned to escort Pope John's car when it left Vatican City were delighted with his spontaneity, they were a little alarmed when in the early days of his pontificate he would try to escape their "protection." He was prevailed upon to conform to the established tradition but used the situation as a lesson in obedience and self-discipline. "Frankly, I would rather do without you," he told them, "but you and I are both subject to rules and regulations and we must try to make the best of it."

✠

A smiling Cardinal Roncalli, surrounded by the Venetian crowds, watched with amusement as a particularly stout citizen rushed to the edge of the throng and worked his bulky way through the group until he reached the center where, to the delight of the audience, he almost fell breathlessly into the arms of the Patriarch. Trying to spare the man any further indignity, Roncalli said sympathetically, "You know the Lord is bound to be particularly tolerant with us fat men."

In the Vatican gardens there is a miniature reproduction of the grotto of Lourdes where Pope Pius XII often went to say his rosary in the late afternoon, always leaving the garden at five o'clock in his usual punctilious way. The papal gendarmes who patrol the territory never expected to see anyone after five o'clock other than an occasional late working gardener or another gendarme. A few weeks after his election Pope John, strolling in the evening after the Angelus, surprised one of the policemen sitting on the ground in a section of the garden with his uniformed unbuttoned. The first indication the sprawled gendarme had of anyone's presence was the resonant voice of the new Pope saying, "Excuse me, may I go up this way?" The astonished guard blurted out a series of sounds that were meant to be permission and apology and John continued his quiet walk through his tiny kingdom.

John once spoke of his famous predecessor, Pope Pius X. "They used to say of him: he may be Pope but he certainly is a fine figure of a man. What can they say about me? A fine figure of a man he certainly isn't, but he has an honest face."

Only a little more than four months after the liberation of Paris, Archbishop Roncalli was appointed papal nuncio, arriving in the city on New Year's Eve, 1944. The excitement of a recently occupied capital city must have been stimulating to a man who had spent the war years in the neutral country of Turkey. He presented himself to a flustered and probably over-worked minor official in an unimposing office. Someone, perhaps a thoughtful secretary, had put a small bouquet of flowers in a vase on the man's desk and sensing his embarrassment Archbishop Roncalli said: "I love everything beautiful and gay God has created, like these flowers which I'm sure were put here for my welcome. I am nuncio only by a series of accidents so please don't bother yourself about all this."

On St. Stephen's Day, the day after Christmas and only a few weeks after his coronation, he went to visit the prisoners in the Regina Coeli prison. Before his coming the officials had arranged a special section of the prison where certain well-screened inmates had been brought and the Pope greeted them cheerfully and gave them his blessing. Then he noticed that there were other prisoners restrained behind bars. "Open the gates," he said. "Don't bar me from them. All of these men are children of the Lord." Then he walked among all the prisoners. "You couldn't come to see me," John said, "so I came to see you." He startled his aides by telling the prisoners that one of his own relatives had served a jail term for hunting without a license. "He was caught by the carabinieri," said the Pope, "and sent to jail for a month." (The Vatican newspaper, *L'Osservatore Romano,* put it more formally in an edition a day or so later—"His Holiness," the paper said, "recalled the bad impression he received as a boy when someone close to him, though in no serious way and though unintentionally, transgressed the law.") John's kind and fatherly attention moved the prisoners to tears and applause. "At this rate," said one prison official, "he can wipe crime off the face of the earth."

At diplomatic receptions in Paris, Archbishop Roncalli excelled in preserving that graceful and easy bearing which is the hallmark of the experienced ambassador. At one reception he was approached by an over-zealous and perhaps overstimulated guest who insisted on having the Archbishop declare himself on the religious merits of a particular situation. "Please," the Archbishop held up a restraining hand. "I never discuss religion at cocktail parties."

✠

John was proud of his family's poverty. He considered it a precious heritage and he often cautioned his relatives against forsaking their humble way of life. Their poverty was not the cruel and oppressive poverty which is the lot of so many Italians but it was real poverty nonetheless. There are no photographs of the Roncallis as children because John's father could not afford even the simplest camera. When he was Patriarch of Venice he recalled his boyhood. "We were poor but happy. It never occurred to us that we lacked anything and really we didn't. Ours was a dignified and happy poverty."

The warm and direct approach of Archbishop Roncalli is nowhere better illustrated than in his meeting with a group of French intellectual and political leaders, most of them not Catholic. "After all," he said with a great shrug, "what is it that really separates us but our ideas and what are ideas among friends?"

When Pope John in making his first appointment chose his good friend and private secretary, young Monsignor Capovilla, as *coppiere* (an honorary post in the papal household) Monsignor Mario Nasalli Rocca di Corneliano objected to the choice, stating that traditionally the *coppiere* had come from the nobility, Nasalli Rocca being himself a nobleman. It may have been this objection which made Capovilla sadly suggest that he return to Venice with Guido Gusso, the Chauffeur who had also accompanied Pope John from Venice. Pope John's reply was typical: "I have never much cared for these names that have a *di* attached to them. Besides, if you two go I'll go back to Venice too."

Visitors to Vatican City are usually impressed by the magnificently uniformed Swiss Guards who for the past four hundred years have guarded the person of the Pope, the exits of the Apostolic Palace to the city and all entrances to the papal apartments. Few, however, understand the devotion and dedication these men have to their duties, and the religious conviction that leads them to seek this more than ordinarily disciplined soldier's life. Pope John XXIII shortly after his election to the papacy met with his Swiss Guards in the customary formal audience. After the audience, the Pope joined them quite informally with a cup of tea. "We see each other every day," he said to them, "but we never get a chance to talk—you because of discipline and I because of protocol. I think it's time we got better acquainted."

Almost immediately after his election Pope John wished to make a telephone call, perhaps to his relatives or possibly to his patriarchate in Venice. A repairman was summoned to make the connection, all communication with the outside world having been cut off according to conclave rules. As the technician worked patiently and the newly elected Pope waited with equal patience the silence grew uncomfortably long and Pope John, not to hurry the workman but out of sympathy, said, "How are things going?" "Badly, badly, Your Eminence," the repairman told him. From the man's tone and address, it was obvious he was unaware that the Cardinal from Venice was the new successor to Peter, and that he was not referring merely to the work at hand. Under gentle questioning he told a familiar and sad story of a large family and little pay—the common lot at the time of the devoted laborers of Vatican City. Eventually the line to the North was available and the workman prepared to leave. After thanking him for his work the newly elected Pope said,

"Just between us, I'm not 'Your Eminence,' any longer; I'm the Pope."

The man's surprise was probably increased when, within a few months, there was a whopping 25 to 40 per cent increase in pay for all employees of Vatican City. The people in charge of Vatican finances explained to the Holy Father that this raise in pay could only be met by cutting back the Holy See's direct contributions to charity and that this just didn't seem feasible at the time. "That's too bad," replied Pope John. "Then we'll just have to cut them. This raise is simple justice, and justice comes before charity."

A few men of learning in the Vatican still found it difficult to understand how some simple laborers could be raised to the equivalent of fifty dollars a week. Cardinal Tardini, the secretary of state, explained it for them: "Pope John said that one man's learning certainly calls for reward but another's problem can be even more urgent—a half-dozen mouths to feed! There were a good fourteen under his own roof. He knows all about the beauties of family life!"

The visits to the slum areas of Rome were perhaps the most pastoral and surprising things undertaken by John after his election to the Papacy. The poor who made their homes in these honeycombs of poverty couldn't believe that "il Papa" was really coming to them, but as the word spread from the parish priests to one house, then to another, the anticipation grew and the preparations became more and more frantic. How show their gratitude? How make festive the grim face of their poverty? They covered the nakedness of their want and hunger by whatever was at hand: bedspreads, curtains, flags were hung from every window. And when he came—as he did to "Tiburtina the Third," one of Rome's more squalid regions—the people came to the church shouting and cheering in their excitement. Pope John's face was clouded for a moment and he raised his finger to his lips in the traditional appeal for silence. "I must compliment you on your obedience," he said as the crowd grew quiet. Then he went on with a little sermon reminding them that they must come to church often, even when he was not there and that "in church you must learn two things, prayer and silence."

As papal nuncio to France Archbishop Roncalli visited more religious houses than one would think possible. Among these groups of religious were the Sisters of Nevers where St. Bernadette Soubirous had spent her life after the Apparitions at Lourdes. When he granted the Sisters of Nevers an audience as Pope John he remembered they also had a growing community in Venice. "They have enlarged it here and enlarged it there until finally the good sisters had to stop because as you know Venice is surrounded by water and they ran the risk of falling in."

When Cardinal Roncalli was Patriarch of Venice he established more than thirty new parishes and took an active and keen interest in their progress. He never neglected the old parishes of the city and his bulky figure was a familiar sight on the public motor launches as he went from one section of the city to the other visiting his priests, "not as a policeman," one young priest has remarked, "but rather as a father." From time to time he found things not quite to his satisfaction and with quiet humor he would remind the guilty pastor that "this is what happens when little boys are in charge."

After the active life of travel and contact with all classes of people he had enjoyed in the diplomatic corps, John XXIII found the comparative inactivity and isolation of the papacy an irksome burden. Once an ambassador from one of the South American countries was received with his family before returning to their homeland. Pope John discussed their studies with the children and then asked the oldest boy: "Where are you going to spend your summer holiday?" "We are all flying home," the boy told him. "How lucky you are to be able to fly about the world like birds," Pope John said. "Only your poor Pope is locked up in the Vatican. Maybe you will come to see me again. You see, I am always here," he added sadly.

In one of his audiences Pope John said, "I, who have come to the pontificate at such an advanced age, hope to have at least the time given to St. Agatho. There are so many things to do."

To the diligent who looked in reference libraries the similarities between these two Popes were interesting. Agatho had in the 7th century sent legates to preside in his place at the Council of Constantinople, being too advanced in age to make the journey himself and was known for his diplomacy, his affability and his great charity.

Commenting once on the hospitality and charity of a Jesuit Superior he had met in Spain, Pope John told of the Superior's insistence on preparing a soup for him with his own hands—a specialty of the country. "His theology was brilliant," the Pope said, "but his cookery was a disaster. I was sick for days." Then he went on to praise the impulsive charity that gave the impetus to attempt the thing which could give his guest pleasure. "The outcome was unimportant," John explained.

John was once asked about his plans for the Church and his purpose in summoning all of the bishops to meet in Rome for the Ecumenical Council. "What do we intend to do?" he said, walking across the room. Throwing open the window he continued: "We intend to let in a little fresh air."

✠

Most Catholic tourists have noticed with affectionate amusement how nuns, so self-effacing and retiring in their everyday life, are capable of forming a flying wedge to reach the front row at any place of pilgrimage. This habit did not escape the twinkling eye of Pope John. At one of his public audiences he noticed the numbers of nuns in the audience of more than 10,000 persons and gently teased them: "Sisters are always so quiet in the convent," he said, "but when they go out they are full of enthusiasm and are always found right up in front."

"The amazing thing about the Pope," a Vatican monsignor said, "is that everyone thinks he is on their side. People come to him all steamed up and walk away smiling."

Cardinal Ottaviani, the leader of the conservative bishops, feeling that things were going against him, went one afternoon to see Pope John to lodge a complaint. The Pope, alone in his library, listened sympathetically, then, taking his old friend by the arm, led him to the window and the two looked out at the sunlight glinting on the tile roofs of Rome. "The city is so beautiful," John murmured. "The sunset tonight will be marvelous." Ottaviani went away, feeling that the Pope had entirely understood him.

"Is it not true," a French statesman asked Roncalli in Paris, "that your Church is favorably inclined to the Popular Republican Movement because so many Catholics are members?" "Monsieur," the nuncio replied, "you must be aware that during Passiontide in our Church all of our statues are covered with a violet veil. I hope that you will permit a papal representative to cover himself with such a veil during an election campaign."

Pope John explained to the Cardinals who had elected him his reason for choosing the name 'John' for his papal title. "It is a name," he said, "which is so dear to me because first of all it was my father's name. It is also the name of the parish church where I was baptized, the name of numberless cathedrals throughout the world and the name of our own Basilica. It reminds us of John the Baptist and that other John who said: 'my children love one another.' There have been twenty-two Popes of this name whose legitimacy is beyond doubt and most of them had a very short reign. Altogether we would prefer to hide our own insignificance behind the great procession of Popes bearing the name of 'John'."

The thousand or more residents of Vatican City who were used to the clock-like regularity of Pius XII's schedule were astonished in the early days of John's pontificate to look up from their various occupations and see the Holy Father walking among them, relaxed and cheerful, listening to stories about their families, giving advice or consolation and encouragement, "as though a country curate had dropped in for a talk," one worker said.

The Leonardo da Vinci Airport is the great air terminal for Rome and John one day decided, after a round of visiting city parishes, to have his driver take him on a sight-seeing tour to the airport. The papal Mercedes-Benz with the famous license plates—SCV-1—arrived just as a flight of tourists from the Philippines touched down. Seeing the Pope standing in the car with the open roof, the tourists crowded around and John talked to them briefly in Italian. How much of the Pope's language they understood is not known but several of the group, when the Pope's car drove down the highway toward Rome, made their way to the terminal again and asked if it was Pope John's custom to meet all tourists arriving at the airport or only those from Catholic countries.

Yousef Karsh of Ottawa has photographed most of the great men and women of contemporary times. His photographic portraits tell their own stories, but each picture has its interesting legend. The wonderful bull-dog determination Mr. Karsh was able to capture in his famous portrait of Winston Churchill was the result of the photographer's having snatched the Prime Minister's cigar from his hand. When Pope John sat for his portrait by Mr. Karsh the humor and benevolence of the new Pope were quickly apparent as the Holy Father remarked, "The Lord knew from all eternity I was going to be Pope and you'd think he would have made me more photogenic."

✠

Cardinal Roncalli always thought of himself as first of all a priest, not as a diplomat or a patriarch. His secretaries in Venice sometimes resented the number of visitors he received, but he insisted that all callers be admitted. "Let them come in," he would say, "they may want to confess." Later as Pope he said, "I wish to meet everyone who wants to see me. No one should be stopped at my door."

Well-bred tourists in Italy have often been shocked by the lack of good taste their fellow-tourists have shown in the matter of dress, and the Patriarch of Venice, whose jurisdiction includes Italy's famous Lido, spoke of this with barbed wit in one summer sermon. "People need not come to Italy in furs or woolens. They can come dressed in modern American silk, fresh and soft, which is a veritable refrigerator at low cost. Italy, on the other hand, is not on the equator, and even there, by the way, lions wear their coats, and crocodiles are covered with their most precious hides."

He once wrote: "Authoritarianism truly suffocates truth by . . . rigid exterior discipline . . . It arrests lawful initiative and is incapable of listening for it confuses inflexibility with firmness. Paternalism is a counterfeit paternity. It takes its objects into custody in order to preserve its power of authority. It makes its liberality felt by everyone, but fails to respect the rights of its subordinates. It speaks in a tone of protection and refuses to accept collaboration."

The Secretary of the Vatican Council, Archbishop Pericle Felici, wrote an article for *L'Osservatore Romano* describing the preparations for assembling the documents relating to the Council's opening session. Pope John had in the preceding months written and spoken to many persons outlining his ideas and two volumes of the preparatory acts were devoted to John's speeches and writings. When Archbishop Felici brought these two volumes in to the papal office Pope John, leafing through the first book, said to his friend: "I see that you have gathered the smallest leaves which have fallen from the tree."

When it was pointed out to Pope John that some members of the Curia thought his desire for a free and unhindered council of the world's bishops a threat to their authority, the Holy Father showed his characteristic but charitable toughmindedness. He had made a wise decision, he knew, and he intended to see it through. "They are men of zeal, I'm sure," he said. "But they are not running the Church. I'm in charge here and I won't allow anyone to stop the momentum of the council."

In his discourse at the opening of the Vatican Council Pope John expressed a holy hope for all men when he said, "we sometimes have to listen, much to our regret, to the voices of persons . . . not much endowed with a sense of discretion or measure . . . they can see nothing in these modern times but prevarication and ruin. They say that our age in comparison with past ages is getting worse . . . but we must disagree with those prophets of doom who are always forecasting disaster . . . In the present order of things Divine Providence is leading us to a new view of human relations which by men's own efforts, even beyond their very expectations, are directed towards the fullfillment of God's superior and inscrutable designs . . ."

When the new Pope received the first homage of the College of Cardinals each cardinal embraced him and kissed his hand but, to their quiet surprise, he would not allow them to kiss his slippered foot according to a centuries-old custom. They were further pleased when the Chinese Cardinal Tien, who had been seriously injured in an automobile accident shortly before the conclave, was brought into the Sistine Chapel in a wheel-chair. Pope John quickly left his throne and hurried to embrace the old prelate.

As Apostolic Delegate in Istanbul, Bishop Roncalli's support was sought by two quarreling French factions—the followers of DeGaulle and the followers of Marshal Petain. One French priest, an ardent Gaullist, pleaded with Roncalli to declare for the French government-in-exile but the delegate, after hearing his impassioned argument, sat for some time in silence. At length he spoke:

"I read in the Bible that the patriarch Jacob also had sons who disagreed among themselves. But he, the father, *rem tacitus considerabat*—considered the matter in silence."

✠

Nothing gave John so much pleasure as the sight of hundreds of thousands of his children gathered in the great square of St. Peter's within the encircling arms of Bernini's colonnade. The night of October 11, 1962, at the end of the first day of the Council, nearly half a million people crowded into the piazza to see the torchlit basilica and the Holy Father watched in delight from his balcony. "Dear children, dear children," he cried to the throng, "I hear your voices. Look there!" He pointed to the bright moon. "See, even the moon has come to join our celebration."

In the course of the first session of the Council it was plain that the majority of the bishops and cardinals did not agree with the ultra-conservative position of Cardinal Ottaviani. Cardinal Ottaviani was particularly displeased with the debate on the proposal entitled "The Sources of Revelation."

He went to Pope John and complained about the dissension and indicated that a quiet word from the Pope could put an end to further dissension and discussion. John is reported to have said, "Dissension? Don't you remember that at the Council of Trent one Italian bishop tore the beard off a Greek bishop?" Ottaviani hinted that if the arguments continued he might resign to avoid further affronts to his dignity. Pope John quietly replied, "You will stay. There will be no resignations."

In his best known Encyclical, *Pacem in Terris,* Pope John said:

"Men's common interests make it imperative that at long last a world-wide community of nations be established . . .

"Man has the right to live. He has the right to bodily integrity and to the means necessary for the proper development of life, particularly food, clothing, shelter, medical care, rest, and, finally, the necessary social services. Consequently he has the right to be looked after in the event of ill-health; disability stemming from his work; widowhood; old age; enforced unemployment; or whenever through no fault of his own he is deprived of the means of livelihood.

"Man has, moreover, a natural right to be respected. He has a right to his good name. He has a right to freedom in investigating the truth and—within the limits of the moral order and the common good—to freedom of speech and publication, and to freedom to pursue whatever profession he may choose. And he has, besides this, the right to be accurately informed about public events . . . The worker is entitled to a wage determined by the precepts of justice. This needs stressing. The amount a worker receives must be sufficient, in proportion to available funds, to allow him and his family a standard of living consistent with human dignity . . .

"Every human being has the right to freedom of movement and of residence within the boundaries of his own State. When there are just reasons in favor of it he must be permitted to emigrate to other countries and take up residence there. The fact that he is a citizen of a particular State does not deprive him of membership in the human family nor of citizenship in that universal society—the common, world-wide fellowship of men . . . Man's personal dignity involves his right to take an active part in public life and to make his own contribution to the common welfare of his fellow citizens . . . As a human person he is entitled to the legal protection of his rights, and such protection must be effective, unbiased and strictly just . . .

"To claim one's rights and ignore one's duties, or only half fulfill them, is like building a house with one hand and tearing it down with the other . . . There is nothing human about a society that is welded together by force . . .

"Since all peoples have either attained political independence or are on the way to attaining it, soon no nation will rule over another and none will be subject to an alien power . . . the long-standing inferiority complex of certain classes because of their economic and social status, sex or position in the State, and the corresponding superiority complex of other classes, is rapidly becoming a thing of the past . . . Any government which refused to recognize human rights or acted in violation of them, would not only fail in its duty; its decrees would be wholly lacking in binding force . . . Truth calls for the elimination of every form of racial discrimination and the consequent recognition of the inviolable principle that all States are by nature equal in dignity . . . Some nations may have attained to a superior degree of scientific, cultural and economic development. But that does not entitle them to exert unjust political domination over other nations. It means that they have to make a greater contribution to the common cause of social progress . . .

✠

"Today the universal common good presents us with problems which are world-wide in their dimensions; problems therefore which cannot be solved except by a public authority with power, organization and means co-extensive with these problems, and with a world-wide sphere of activity. The moral order itself consequently demands the establishment of some such general form of public authority . . . It is our earnest wish that the United Nations Organization may be able progressively to adapt its structure and methods of operation to the magnitude and nobility of its tasks. May the day be not long delayed when every human being can find in this organization an effective safeguard of his personal rights . . .

Cardinal Roncalli once reproved a young priest in Venice for having given one hundred lire (approximately fifteen cents) to a poor person. "A gift must be of some use," he pointed out. He advised the young man that, times being what they were, he should have given the poor man at least one thousand lire.

John had a Roman turn of mind and quoted to a visitor the old story about the unhappy discrepancy between religious belief and moral practice in the Eternal City. There are two statues in the Piazza San Pietro, one of St. Peter, another of St. Paul. St. Peter's hand points down. "Here is where the laws are made," he seems to say. St. Paul's hand points toward the horizon. "But there," the Romans say Paul is telling them, "is where the laws are obeyed."

✠

To Pope John the heritage of truth which has come down from Apostolic times to today was not only a sacred treasure to be guarded zealously but a living thing which, he told the Council, "should be studied and expounded through modern research and modern scholarly disciplines . . . The Church must ever look to the present, to new conditions and new ways of life in the modern world . . . Our duty is not only to guard this precious treasure, as if it were concerned only with antiquity, but to dedicate ourselves with an earnest will and without fear to that work which our era demands of us . . . The substance of the ancient doctrine of the deposit of faith is one thing. The way in which it is presented is another."

Pope John's hospitality extended to many groups of entertainers. Among those he received was a traveling circus, complete with animals. He patted a lion cub named "Dolly" and ordered her to "behave here. You know the only other lion of our acquaintance is the calm lion of St. Mark."

At the close of World War I, Chaplain Roncalli returned to Bergamo and was given permission to open a center for students attending public schools. At the new center they were given spiritual instruction and, more often than not, material assistance. "Reasons affecting the stomach are very close to those touching the spirit or the heart," Roncalli explained. While in Bergamo he also founded an association of Catholic University Women and served as moderator for a Students' Union at the Palazzo Asperti. He had placed a full-length mirror just inside the main doorway with the inscription, "Know Thyself", hoping to make the students aware of the importance of making a good appearance. His enthusiasm for the young remained with him all his life and probably to some extent explained his own youthful thinking and infectious joy.

He told a group of international bankers in May of 1962: "The problems of the Pope are moral problems and religious problems. One might believe that they would not directly interest professionals in a branch of human activity as specialized as yours. But your presence here proves exactly the contrary. It is true that every activity in this world, whatever its aim, has a humane, an intellectual and a moral aspect, and it is to your credit that you recognize this fact—as you have proved by coming here to this house where everyone feels at home since it is the house of the common father of all the faithful."

A few weeks after John XXIII's coronation a group of tourists in St. Peter's Square stared in disbelief when through the center doors of the basilica walked the new Pope and three or four companions. The Pope of Rome traditionally enters St. Peter's carried on the *sedia gestatoria* but John explained that it had been quite some time since he had seen the great church as the ordinary tourist sees it and he felt that this time would be as good as any other to make the visit.

After the first session of the Vatican Council John XXIII, although pleased that a start had been made, was fearful that the opposition of the more conservative cardinals in the Curia would hinder the progress he hoped for in the next session. In the spring of 1963 he wrote to one of these cardinals: "Venerable Brother, we are in continuous pain and suffering at the constant way in which you have organized your life and office to maintain a continued opposition to our deepest wishes, and we only pray that God, our common Father, may either shed light in your heart or take us away from the pain of conflict with you . . ."

"When people go too far," he once wrote to a friend, "it is advisable to apply a little ear-tweaking."

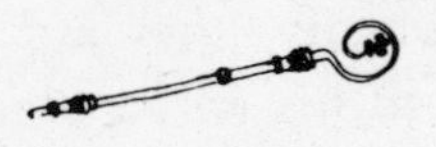

For generations Catholics had thought of the Pope as a prisoner of the Vatican but no Pope did so much to correct the illusion as John XXIII. At the beginning of his pontificate he traveled about Rome so much that the foreign correspondents in Rome affectionately dubbed him "Johnny Walker" and "the Harry Truman of the Popes." The Rome police, who were accustomed to elaborate preparations when a pope left the Vatican, finally abandoned hope of such notice from Pope John's staff after he had made twenty trips outside the Vatican in four months and they stationed two motorcycle policemen at the exit of the Vatican Palace. The Holy Father's trips were not inspired by mere whim as the press soon discovered. Most were visitations to slum parishes, "I came to you," he would explain, "because I thought the meeting of the shepherd with his sheep should not be limited to the center of the city."

Once, when he was unaccounted for for more than an hour and a half, he was found quietly visiting his fellow priests at a home for aged clergymen, miles from the formality of Vatican City.

When French President Auriol told Cardinal-designate Roncalli that he would like to present the red biretta symbolic of his new ecclesiastical office to the Apostolic Delegate, Roncalli jovially recalled the remark of a certain Father Talpa, a disciple of St. Philip, which he remembered from his seminary days: "When they speak ill of you—it is true. When they pay you compliments—they are joking."

After a brief visit to his native Bergamo he returned to

Paris to receive the Cardinal's hat. A short time before the ceremony he wrote: "It is neither a sacrament nor a sacramental; and yet it is a kind of sign that providence has responsibilities in store for me which will require me to give a serious account of myself."

✠

Speaking to the observer delegates to the Council the day after the opening session, Pope John shared with them some intimate recollections of his experiences of that day. "I devoted all my attention to the immediate duty of preserving recollection, of praying and giving thanks to God. But my eye from time to time ranged over the multitude of sons and brothers and suddenly, as my glance rested upon your group, on each of you personally, I drew a special comfort from your presence . . . It is now for the Catholic Church to bend herself to her work with calmness and generosity. It is for you to observe her with renewed and friendly attention."

In January, 1954, when he was the Patriarch of Venice, Cardinal Roncalli gave a series of lectures on Christian unity in the great hall of St. Basso. "The road to unity between the different Christian creeds," he said, "is love—so little practiced on either side."

Whether John's patience was the result of his peasant origins or the natural companion to his advanced years, he evidenced a great patience with the proceedings of the Council as the debates continued and the weeks passed. Some of the bishops felt that further discussions were useless and on one occasion a group of Eastern bishops called on Pope John. He sensed their impatience with the progress of the debates and decided to test their reactions. "You with the beard," he suddenly said to a tall prelate with a particularly long beard, "what do you think of this council?" The bishop answered almost as informally as he had been addressed: "Not much, we're not doing anything." Pope John thought a moment and then said, "No, you're wrong. You sit down there in St. Peter's and you listen. I sit up here in my apartment and listen in on television—and we both learn something."

Pope John's brother, Zaverio, was visiting the Pope just prior to the Council's opening session and the farmer from the northern hills was interested in all of the preparations that were being made in the great basilica of St. Peter. "You're going to have an enormous number of bishops here, aren't you?" Zaverio asked his brother. "What will you do at the Council?" John reminded Zaverio of the farming they had done together. "You know how a farmer hitches two horses to his plough and then ploughs the uplands and the plains? Well, it's a kind of trinity of work. I'm the ploughman, the bishops are the horses and together we can plough the uplands and plains of this world for Christ."

Some career churchmen in Rome were appalled at the open and public manner in which John XXIII seemed to accept the political and religious ideologies of all men. One was bold enough to caution the Pope to use a little more discretion than he was showing. With a shrug and an innocent smile, John answered his critic: "Sono tutti i miei figlioli, non e vero? (All of them are my children—isn't that true?)"

To Cardinal Ottaviani, whose coat of arms bears the Latin inscription *Semper Idem* ("Always the Same"), the theological scholarship of German Jesuit Father Karl Rahner was not so much an answer to the needs of modern pastoral life as the seeds of heresy and revolution. The cardinal asked the Pope to send Rahner back to Innsbruck. "Well now, Eminenza," John replied, "I think you would do better to discuss Father Rahner with Cardinal Koenig (of Vienna). I wouldn't think of telling a bishop how to manage his priests.

Besides this, if Father Rahner came as Cardinal Koenig's theologian he's the man to send him away."

✠

From the moment of his election, Pope John was aware that his reign would in all probability be a short one. "One who becomes pope at seventy-eight does not have a great future," he dryly told a group of friends. But he added, "One who trusts in God has no reason to fear anything—not even the surprise of death."

When a band of seminarians came to congratulate him on his eighty-first birthday he cheerfully told them, "Any day is a good day to be born and any day is a good day to die. We have arrived at the start of our eighty-second year. Will we see it through to the end? It is of no great concern."

A short time later, he was troubled by the recurrence of a stomach disorder. He told one of the doctors, "They say I have a tumor. Very well then, God's will be done. But you mustn't worry about me. My bags are packed and I'm ready to go." His condition became steadily worse and he was forced to take to his bed. The world learned from the medical bulletins that hope for his recovery had been abandoned.

The Pope asked to receive the last sacraments of the Church and Bishop Peter van Lierde brought Communion to him. "I have been able to follow my death step by step," he told one of his attending monsignors; "now I am going sweetly toward the end."

Cardinal Montini arrived with the Pope's three brothers and his sister. About 3 o'clock in the morning John awoke from his coma and looked at his brother. "Is that you, Zaverio?" he asked. "Don't look at me as if I were a ghost. The Lord has allowed me to see you again and wanted me to return to myself so that I could enjoy this long agony. Yesterday I was dead, today I am alive . . . I can leave now with an untroubled conscience. Soon I will be in Heaven where our parents are waiting for me. What a celebration when we meet Battista and Marian!"

A short time later the Pope recognized a grandchild. "Ah, here's the man of letters in the family," he joked. "Well, maybe not the first because that's me."

Those around the death-bed were moved to tears at the courage and composure of the dying man who seemed more concerned for their comfort than for his own. His private secretary, young Monsignor Capovilla, knelt weeping near the bed. The Pope beckoned to him. Capovilla bent over to hear the Pope whisper, "When this is all over be sure to go and see your mother." Later, in an agony of pain, he murmured, "I offer myself as a sacrifice on the altar for the Church, for the Council and for peace." Frequently he was heard to say "*Ut unum sint* (that all may be one)." A small reserve of strength returned and the Pope called some of the older cardinals to the room. "I am sorry to be going," he said. When his brothers and his sister approached the bedside he embraced each of them and bade them good-bye reminding them that he would soon be joining their parents.

An evening Mass for the Pope was celebrated outdoors, in the great piazza of St. Peter's. 75,000 people crowded the area to pray for the dying pontiff. As Cardinal Traglia finished the Mass, word reached the throng that good Pope John had just died—at eleven minutes before eight, Monday evening, June 3, 1963.

Norman Cousins, editor of the *Saturday Review*, described his visit with Pope John in the following way:

"He leaned forward in his chair and smiled. 'When I meet a person and talk to him privately, I try to put him at ease by reminding him that I am the same as he is. I have two eyes, a nose—a very large nose—mouth, two ears, and so forth. Even so, people sometimes remain rigid and uncommunicative. You must feel completely relaxed. We will talk as man to man.' And again he smiled.

"I handed him a letter expressing the President's concern and good wishes for his health.

" 'I get many messages these days from people who pray that my illness is without great pain. Pain is no foe of mine. I have memories. Wonderful memories. I have lived a long life and I have much to look back upon. These memories give me great joy now and fill my life. There is really no room for the pain.

" 'There is so much to think back upon. When I was young, I was an apostolic Delegate in Bulgaria. I came to know and admire the Slavic peoples. I tried to study the Slavic languages, including the Russian. I never became really proficient but I did learn to read the language to some extent. I am sorry that I never pursued these studies. Do you know the Russian language?'

" 'No.'

" 'A pity. You really ought to learn it. You are much younger than I. It wouldn't take you very long. A very important language. The Russian people, a very wonderful people. We must not condemn them because we do not like their political system. They have a deep spiritual heritage. This they have not lost. We can talk to them. Right now we have to talk to them. We must always try to speak to the good in people. Nothing can be lost by trying. Everything can be lost if men do not find some way to work together to save the peace. I am not afraid to talk to anyone about peace on earth. If Mr. Khrushchev were sitting right where you are sitting now, I don't think I would feel uneasy or awkward in talking to him. We both come from small villages. We both have peasant backgrounds. We would understand one another.

" 'Much depends now on keeping open and strengthening all possible lines of communications. During the terrible crisis over Cuba in October, the possibility of a nuclear holocaust became very real. I asked the statesmen to exercise the greatest restraint and to do all that had to be done to reduce the terrible tension. My appeal was given prominent attention inside the Soviet Union. I was glad that this was so. This is a good sign.'

"His voice betrayed his fatigue and general sense of depletion, but he spoke with eagerness. There wasn't too much time left to him personally (our discussion took place in December, 1962), but he was determined to use himself fully as long as he could in the service of world peace. The Holy See might be useful in reducing tensions between the East and West. Therefore it was logical to open up contacts. The Holy See was not attempting to arrogate to itself an unwelcome or unnatural role. But the grimly significant feature of the present world crisis was precisely that there were so many elements of danger and so few elements of control. Any person or agency in a position, near or far, to help strengthen the controls had a positive obligation to do so.

"Did he know that his efforts were likely to be criticized or misconstrued? Certainly, but this was no warrant for lack of initiative or irresponsible inaction. The worst that could be said was that the Pope was taking Christianity literally. He couldn't imagine Jesus concurring in the notion that human security and freedom depended on the manufacture and amassing of hydrogen bombs which, if used, would put a torch to the human nest. The fact that two or more nations, in the act of warring against one another, would in actuality also be at war with the human race—if this fact had no profound moral and spiritual significance, then what fact did?

"This question, along with all the other central questions related to peace and the human future, formed the basis of the historic encyclical, *Peace on Earth,* in April. A few weeks later, the progressive nature of his illness became critical. Even so, he followed events carefully. He looked for evidence that the nations were making progress in organizing their relationships and halting the arms race. He was heartened by the world-wide response to his plea for peace. His hopes were never higher than at the end. Some men will recognize that a claim has thus been laid on them in terms of their own efforts and obligations. The sustaining prospect is that there may be enough of them.

"We live in an age which looks to physical motion for its spectacular achievements. A man encased in a metallic space capsule spinning through outer space; the heart of an atom pried open and releasing vast stores of energy; streams of electrons flashing images of something happening thousands of miles away—these are the main articles of wonder in the modern world. But they do not have the impress on history of an eighty-one-year-old man dying of cancer, using the Papacy to make not just his own church but all churches fully relevant and fully alive in the cause of human unity and peace. Human advocacy harnessed to powerful ideas continues to be the prime power. The peace sought by Pope John need not be unattainable once belief in ideas is put ahead of belief in moving parts."

His Last Letter To His Family

My dear brother Severo. Today is the feast of your great patron—he of your true and proper name, St. Francis Xavier, as our dear "barba"[1] was called and now, happily, our nephew Zaverio.

I think it is three years since I stopped using a typewriter, as I liked so much to do; and if I have decided today to resume the practice and to employ a new machine that is all my own, it is because I have reached the age of eighty. But I continue to be well; and I am starting out again along the good path still in good health, although some little disturbance makes me say that 80 is not 60 nor 50. For now, at least, I can continue the good service of the Lord and of the Holy Church.

This letter which I have chosen to address to you, my dear Severo, as a message intended for everyone—Alfredo, Giuseppino, Assunta, sister-in-law Caterina, your dear Maria, Virgino, and Angelo Ghisleni, as well as all our relatives—I want to be an expression of my affection for all of you, affection ever keen and ever fresh. Though I am engaged, as you know, in a very important service, a service toward which the eyes of the whole world are directed, I cannot forget my beloved relatives, to whom my thoughts turn from day to day.

It gives me pleasure to tell you that since you cannot correspond personally with me as you once could, you can confide

[1] Apparently a nickname for his uncle Zaverio.

everything to Msgr. Capovilla, who is very fond of you and to whom you can say everything just as you would to me.

Please remember that this is one of the very few private letters I have written to any of my family during the past three years of my pontificate; and please sympathize with me if I can do no more, not even with those of my own blood. This sacrifice which I impose upon myself in my relations with you does more honor to you and to me and gains more respect and understanding than you could believe or imagine.

Now the great displays of reverence and affection for the Pope on the occasion of his 80th birthday are coming to an end, and I am glad because I prefer to the praise and best wishes of men the mercy of the Lord who has chosen me for a task so great that I desire Him to sustain me to the end of my life.

My personal tranquillity, which makes so great an impression on the world, consists completely in this: to persevere in obedience as I always have, and not to desire or pray to live longer, not even for one day beyond the time when the angel of death will come to call me and take me to Paradise, as I am confident he will.

That does not keep me from thanking the Lord for having decided to find in Brusico and Colombera[2] the man destined to be called the direct successor of so many popes through 20 centuries, and to take the name of Vicar of Jesus Christ on earth.

Through this call the name Roncalli was brought to the attention, sympathy, and respect of the whole world. And you do well to hold fast to your humility, as I also strive to do, and not to allow yourselves to be carried away by the follies and wiles of the world. The world is interested only in making money—enjoying life and having its way at all costs, even if unfortunately this requires force.

[2] Brusico and Colombera are the names of the two houses in which Pope John lived as a boy.

The 80 years that have gone by tell me, and you too dear Severo, and all of our dear ones, that what counts most is to keep ourselves always well prepared to pass away suddenly; for this is the most important thing: to assure ourselves of eternal life by trusting in the goodness of the Lord, who sees all and provides for all.

I want to express these sentiments to you, my most dear Severo, so that you may pass them on to all our close relatives from Colombera, Gerole, Bonate, Medolago, and wherever they may be, and to those whose exact town I do not know. I leave to your discretion how to go about it. I think that Enrica could help you and Don Battista as well.

Continue loving one another, all you Roncallis who make up new families, and please try to understand if I cannot write to each family. Our Giuseppino is right when he says to his brother the Pope: "Here you are a prisoner of luxury and you cannot do all that you would like."

It gives me joy to recall the names of those who are suffering most among you: dear Maria, your blessed wife, and good Rita, who with her sufferings has assured Paradise for herself and for you two who have helped her with so much charity; sister-in-law Caterina, who always reminds me of her, and our Giovanni who looks down upon us from heaven, together with our Roncalli relatives and other close relatives like those who emigrated to Milan.

I know that you will have to endure some mortification from those who choose to jump to conclusions without good judgment. So it is to have in the family a Pope, to whom the respectful gaze of the whole world turns, and to have his relatives living so modestly, remaining in their social position. But then many know that the Pope, son of humble but honorable people, does not forget anyone, and has and shows a good heart for all his closest relatives; that, besides, his condition is that of nearly all his recent predecessors; and that the honor of a pope is not to make his relatives rich, but only to help them with charity according to their needs and each one's condition.

This is and will be one of the finest and most prized titles of Pope John and of his Roncalli family.

At my death I will not lack the tribute that so honored the holiness of Pius X: *born poor and died poor.*

It is only natural that since I have reached the age of 80, all the others are coming along behind me. Courage, courage! We are in good company. I always keep close by my bed the photograph that gathers together all our dead, with their names written on marble: grandfather Angelo, uncle Zaverio, our venerable parents, our brother Giovanni, sisters Teresa, Ancilla, Maria, and Enrica. Oh, what a wonderful chorus of souls is waiting for us and praying for us! I am always thinking of them. To remember them in prayer gives me courage and fills me with joy in trustful expectation of being united with them all in heavenly and eternal glory.

I bless all of you together, recalling the wives who have come to gladden the Roncalli family or have gone to increase the joy of new families of different names but the same feelings. Oh, the children, the children! What a treasure, and what a blessing!

JOANNES XXIII PP.

Pope John's Last Will and Testament

Venice
June 29, 1954

MY SPIRITUAL TESTAMENT AND LAST WISHES

On the point of presenting myself before the One and Triune Lord who created me, redeemed me, chose me to be his priest and bishop, and covered me with unending graces, I entrust my poor soul to His mercy; I humbly ask pardon for my sins and deficiencies. I offer Him the little good, although petty and imperfect, that with His aid I have succeeded in doing, for His glory, for the service of Holy Church, for the edification of my brethren, begging Him finally to receive me, like a good and kind father, with His Saints into eternal happiness.

I profess once again with all my heart my entire Christian and Catholic faith, my adherence and subjection to the Holy Apostolic and Roman Church, and my complete devotion and obedience to her August Head, the Supreme Pontiff, whom it was my great honor to represent for long years in various regions of the East and West, who at the end chose to have me come to Venice as Cardinal and Patriarch, and whom I have always followed with sincere affection, aside from and above and beyond any dignity conferred upon me. The sense of my own littleness and nothingness has always been my good companion, keeping me humble and calm, and making me employ myself to the best of my ability in a constant exercise of obedience and charity for souls and for the interests of the Kingdom of Jesus, my Lord and my all. To Him be all glory; for me and for my merit, His mercy. *Meritum meum miseratio Domini. Domine, tu omnia nosti: tu scis quia amo Te.*[1] This alone is enough for me.

I ask pardon of those whom I have unwittingly offended, of all to whom I have not been a source of edification. I feel that I have nothing to forgive anyone, for all who have known and dealt with me—including those who have offended me, scorned me, held me in bad esteem (with good reason, for that matter), or have been a source of affliction to me—I regard solely as brothers and benefactors, to whom I am grateful and for whom I pray and always will pray.

Born poor, but of honorable and humble people, I am particularly happy to die poor, having given away, in accordance with the various demands and circumstances of my simple and modest life, for the benefit of the poor and of the Holy Church that had nurtured me, all that came into my hands—which was little enough, as a matter of fact—during the years of my priesthood and episcopacy. Outward appearances of ease and comfort often veiled hidden thorns of distressing poverty and kept me from giving with all the largesse I would have liked. I thank God for this grace of poverty which I vowed in my youth, poverty of spirit as a priest of the Sacred Heart, and real poverty. This grace has sustained me in never asking for anything, neither positions, nor money, nor favors—never, not for myself, nor for my relatives or friends.

To my beloved family *secundum sanguinem*[2]—from whom, in fact, I have received no material wealth—I can leave only a wholehearted and most special blessing, inviting it to main-

[1] My merit is the mercy of the Lord. Lord, thou hast known all things. Thou knowest that I love Thee.
[2] By blood.

tain that fear of God that always made it so dear and beloved to me, simple and modest as it was, without my ever feeling ashamed of it: this is its true title to honor. I have also helped it at times in its more serious needs, as one poor man with the other poor, but without ever removing it from the honorable poverty with which it was content. I pray and always will pray for its prosperity! I am happy to see in its new, vigorous offshoots that strength and loyalty to their fathers' religious tradition which will always be its fortune. My most fervent wish is that none of my relatives and dear ones may miss the joy of that last eternal reunion.

Departing, as I trust, for the roads of Heaven, I salute and thank and bless the many who formed my spiritual family at Bergamo, at Rome, in the East, in France, and at Venice, and who were my fellow-townsmen, benefactors, colleagues, students, aides, friends and acquaintances, priests and laymen, Brothers and Sisters, and for whom, by the disposition of Providence, I was, no matter how unworthy, a colleague, a father, or a pastor.

The goodness directed toward my poor person by all whom I met along my path made my life serene. As I face death, I recall each and every one—those who have preceded me in taking the final step, those who will survive me and who will follow me. May they pray for me. I will repay them from Purgatory or from Paradise, where I hope to be received, I repeat it once again, not because of my merits, but because of the mercy of my Lord.

I remember all and will pray for all. But my children of Venice—the last ones the Lord placed around me, as a final consolation and joy for my priestly life—I want especially to mention as a sign of my admiration, my gratitude, my very special tenderness. I embrace them all in spirit, clergy and laity without exception, as I have loved them without exception as members of the same family, the object of one paternal and priestly care and love. *Pater sancte, serva eos in nomine tuo quos dedisti mihi: ut sint unum sicut et nos.*[3]

At the moment for saying farewell, or better still, *arrivederci,* I once more remind everyone of what counts most in life: blessed Jesus Christ, His Holy Church, His Gospel; and in the Gospel, above all, the *Pater noster* in the spirit and heart of Jesus and the Gospel, the truth and goodness, the goodness meek and kind, active and patient, victorious and unbowed.

My children, my brethren, *arrivederci.* In the name of the Father, of the Son, of the Holy Spirit. In the name of Jesus, our love; of Mary, our and His most sweet Mother; of St. Joseph, my first and specially loved Protector. In the name of St. Peter, St. John the Baptist, St. Mark, St. Lawrence Justinian, and St. Pius X. Amen.

Cardinal Angelo
Giuseppe Roncalli,
patriarch.

(The following additions to the text were all made in his own handwriting.)

. . . These pages that I have written are valid as an attestation of my absolute will in case of my sudden death.
Venice, September 17, 1957.
Angelo Giuseppe Cardinal Roncalli

And they are valid also as a spiritual testament to be added to the provisions of the will joined here under the date of April 30, 1959.

JOANNES XXIII PP.

From Rome, December 4, 1959.

[3] *John* 17, 11. "Holy Father, keep them in thy name whom thou hast given me; that they may be one, as we also are."

MY TESTAMENT

Castelgandolfo
September 12, 1961

Under the dear and trusting auspices of Mary, my heavenly Mother, to whose name is dedicated today's liturgy, and in the eightieth year of my age, I hereby lay down and renew my testament, annulling every other declaration concerning my will made and written prior to this a number of times.

I await and will accept with simplicity and joy the arrival of sister death in all the circumstances with which it will please the Lord to send her to me.

First of all, I ask forgiveness of the Father of mercies *pro innumerabilibus peccatis, offensionibus et negligentiis meis,* as I have so often said and repeated in offering my daily Sacrifice.

For this first grace of Jesus' pardon for all my faults, and of my soul's introduction into blessed and eternal Paradise, I recommend myself to the prayers of all who have followed me and known me during the whole of my life as priest, bishop, and most humble and unworthy Servant of the Servants of the Lord.

Next, my heart leaps with joy to make a fervent, wholehearted renewal of my profession of Catholic, apostolic, and Roman faith. Among the various forms and symbols with which the faith is usually expressed, I prefer the priestly and pontifical "Credo" of the Mass because of its more vast, more sonorous elevation as in union with the universal Church of every rite, of every age, of every region—from the "*Credo in unum Deum, patrem omnipotentem*" to the "*et vitam venturi saeculi.*"

CHRONOLOGY

1881	Angelo Giuseppe Roncalli born, November 25, Sotto il Monte in Province of Bergamo
1892-1900	Seminarian in Bergamo
1900-1904	Seminarian in Rome
1904	Ordained priest in Rome at Church of Santa Maria in Monte Santo, August 15
1905-1914	Private secretary to Bishop of Bergamo, Msgr. Radini-Tedeschi, and professor at seminary in Bergamo
1915-1918	Military service, first as medical orderly, later as army chaplain
1921	Pope Benedict XV assigns Father Roncalli to Propagation of Faith office in Rome
1925	Consecrated bishop; appointed apostolic visitor to Bulgaria
1935	Appointed apostolic delegate to Turkey and to Greece
1944	Appointed papal nuncio to France
1953	Appointed cardinal; three months later named Patriarch of Venice
1958	Elected Pope, October 28
1963	Died, June 3, Vatican City